DEMI'S OPPOSITES

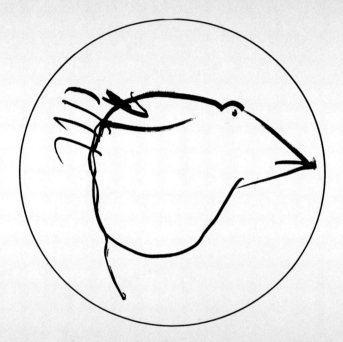

For my nephew,
Richard Morris Hunt (age 2),
who drew this bird

Publishers · Grosset & Dunlap · New York

Copyright © 1987 by Demi. All rights reserved. Published by Grosset & Dunlap, a member of The Putnam Publishing Group, New York. Published simultaneously in Canada. Printed in Italy. Library of Congress Catalog Card Number: 87-80183 ISBN 0-448-18995-X A B C D E F G H I J

DEMI'S
OPPOSITES

An Animal Game Book

OVER/UNDER

Can you tell me this,
I wonder...
Who is over?
Who is under?

If this is something
that you know…
Then who's above
and who's below?

ABOVE/BELOW

OPEN/SHUT
NOISY/QUIET

A noisy mouth
is open, but...
It's quiet
if it is kept shut.

PLAIN/FANCY

These dinosaurs are shaped the same.
But one is fancy, one is plain.

Find this plain dinosaur.

Find this fancy dinosaur.

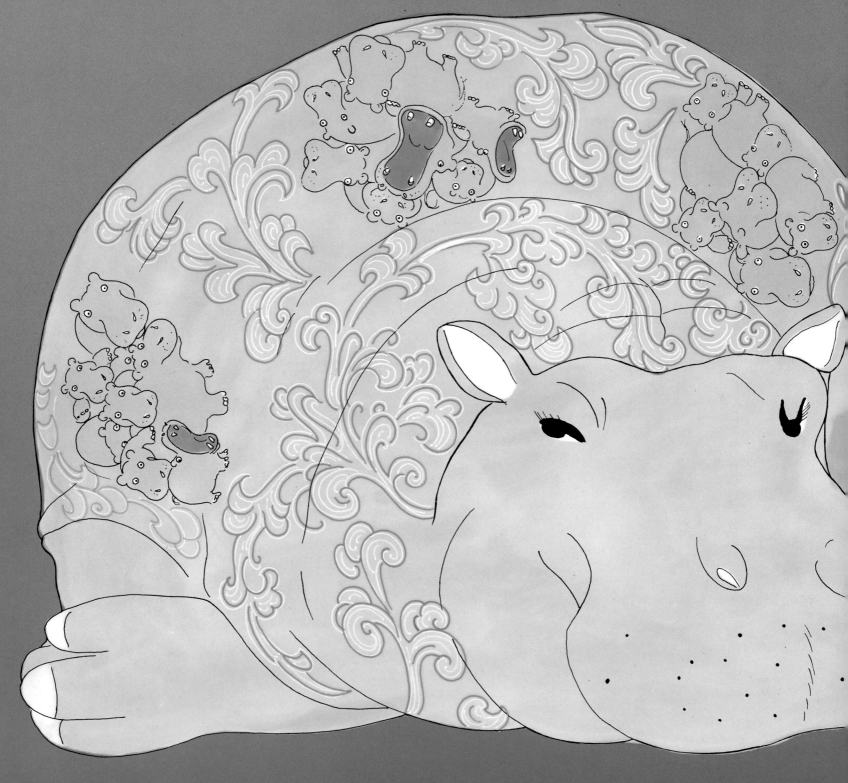

Each hippo looks
just like a sack…
With a face in front
and a tail in back.

Find this hippo facing front.

Find this hippo facing back.

FAT/THIN

Some are fat
and some are thin.
That's the way
it has always been.

COME/GO

These fish see
something
good to eat.
Here they come
to get the treat.

Now the fish have
crumbs to eat.
There they go
in fast retreat.

Find this fish coming.
Find this fish going.

CURLY/STRAIGHT

I think that you can
tell me, surely...

Which grass is straight
and which is curly?

MANY/FEW

These capybaras
say to you...

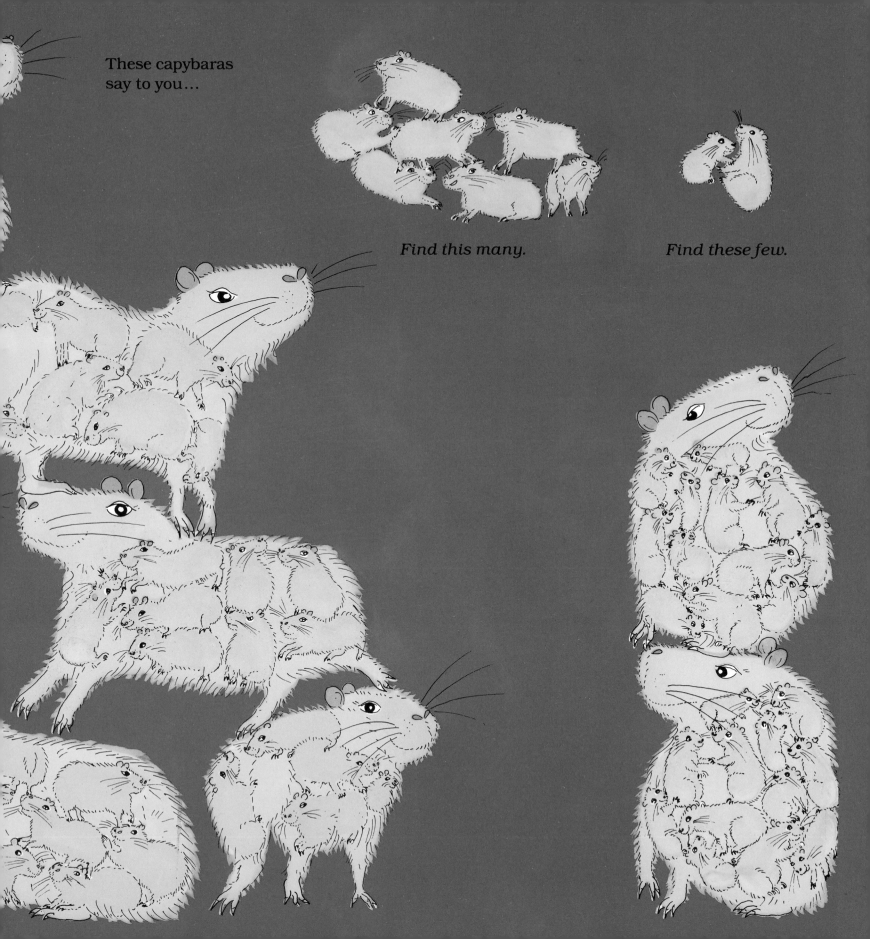

Find this many.

Find these few.

INSIDE/OUTSIDE

Inside the tree
the nest is snug.
But each chick wants
a worm or bug.

Outside the tree
their father seeks
the food to fill
their hungry beaks.

Find this bug inside the tree.
Find this bug outside the tree.

EMPTY/FULL

A hippo stands by an empty sea
with a very full stomach...
How can that be?

He emptied the sea to quench his thirst.
But he filled his poor belly...
I hope it won't burst!

Find this empty bottle.
Find this full bottle.

DIRTY/CLEAN

Who is laughing, who is sad?
Who is crying, who is glad?
Who is dirty, who is clean?
Who is nice and who is mean?

BIG/LITTLE
OLD/YOUNG

Summer, winter, spring or fall,
big or little, large or small…
There is much that someone old
can teach to someone young,
I'm told.

Find this big elephant.
Find this little elephant.

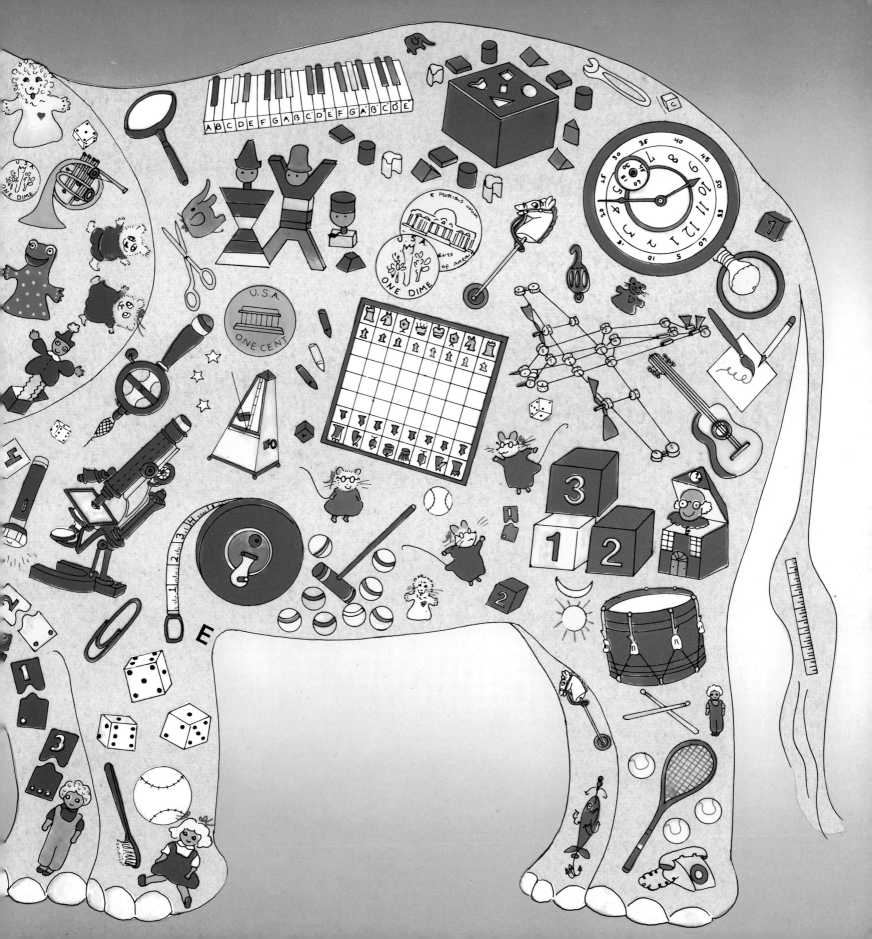

CIRCLE/SQUARE

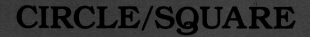

This pony's in the circle
and he's also in the square.

I want you to find him hiding.
Can you tell me where?

AWAKE/ASLEEP

Two lesser red pandas
awake in a heap…
Upon their poor father
who's still fast asleep!

Find this panda asleep.
Find this panda awake.

NEAR/FAR

Some birds are near.
Some birds are far.
It just depends
on where you are.

Find this near bird.
Find this far bird.

UP/DOWN

Whose ears are up?
Whose ears have flopped?
Whose ears are down
because they've dropped?

ALIKE/DIFFERENT

These bears are marching proudly
on a patriotic hike.
One of them is different,
but three are just alike.

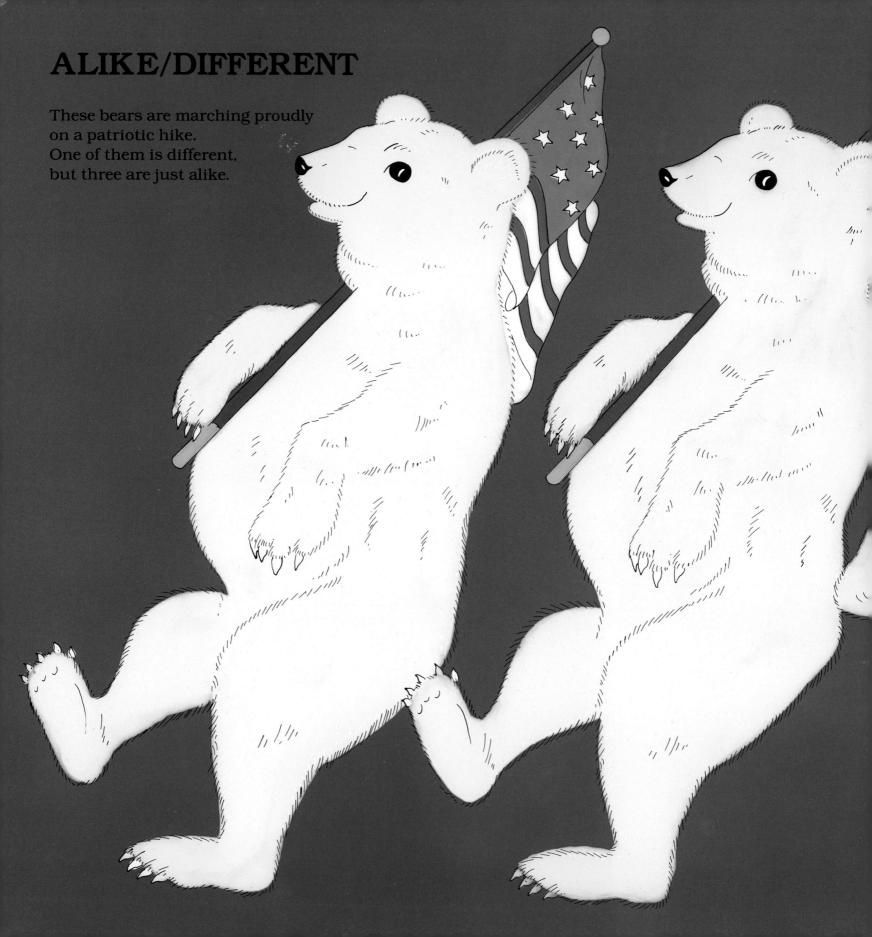

Find this different bear.
Find this different star.

DARK/LIGHT
NIGHT/DAY

In the dark,
most every night,
the screech owl
hunts his prey.

Find this night owl.

But then he is
so tired that
he sleeps
by light of day.

Find this day owl.

RIGHT SIDE UP/UPSIDE DOWN

Who's right side up?
Who's upside down?
Does this question cause a frown?

To the geese
it couldn't be clearer.
The lake is acting as a mirror.

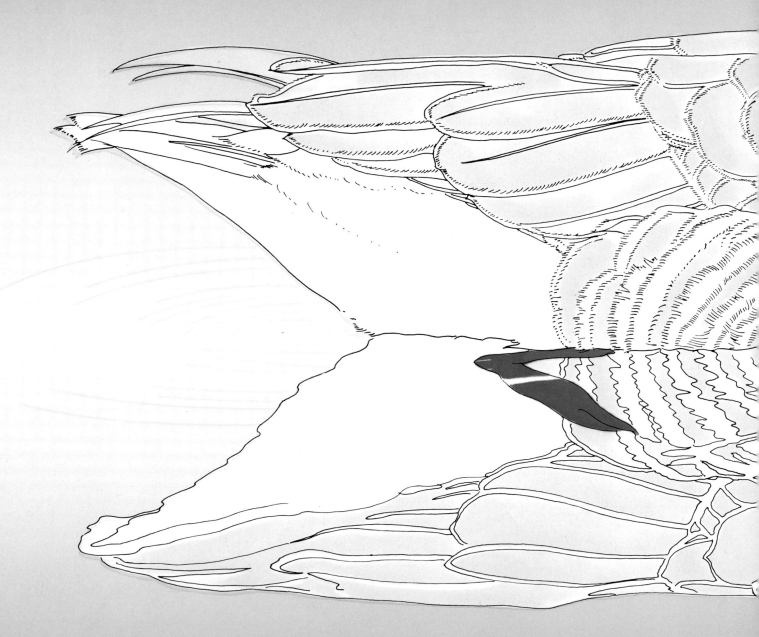

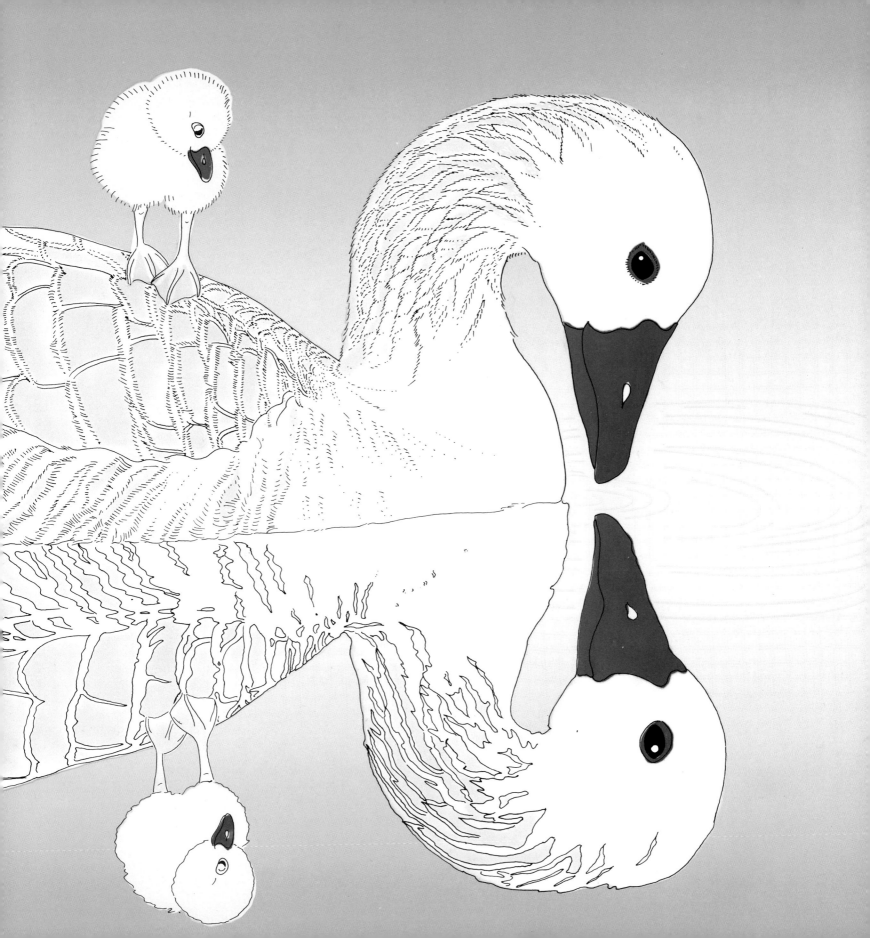

FAST/SLOW

A cheetah's fast.
A snail is slow.
If you could choose,
how would you go?

BLACK/WHITE
LEFT/RIGHT

One llama's black,
one llama's white.
Who's looking left?
Who's looking right?

Find this llama looking left.
Find this llama looking right.

RICH/POOR

The rich cat has
a heap of fish.
The poor cat has
an empty dish.

I know it doesn't
seem quite fair.
The rich cat ought to
learn to share.

BEGINNING

Where's the beginning?
Where's the end?
Can you tell me this,
my friend?

END